MUFFINS

MUFFINS

SIXTY SWEET AND SAVORY
RECIPES...FROM OLD FAVORITES
TO NEW

By Elizabeth Alston

Illustrations by Sally Sturman

Clarkson N. Potter, Inc./Publishers

Published by Clarkson N. Potter, Inc., 201 East 50th Street, New York, New York 10022. Member of the Crown Publishing Group.

Random House, Inc. New York, Toronto, London, Sydney, Auckland

Clarkson N. Potter, Potter, and colophon are trademarks of Clarkson N. Potter, Inc.

Manufactured in the United States of America.

Design by Justine Strasberg

Library of Congress Cataloging-in-Publication Data
Alston, Elizabeth.
  Muffins: sixty sweet and savory recipes from old favorites to new.
  Includes index.
  1. Muffins.   I. Title.   II. Title: Muffins: 60 sweet and savory recipes from old favorites to new.
TX769.A49   1984   641.8'15   84-18372
ISBN 0-517-55587-5

     30 29 28 27 26

CONTENTS

ACKNOWLEDGMENTS

Special thanks to recipe development associate Miriam Rubin, to nutritionist Elizabeth Hanna Schwartz for help with the special diet recipes, and to Deborah Mintcheff.

The English Muffin recipe on page 67 was adapted from one developed by Diana Sturgis and used by permission, *Food and Wine*, May 1982, copyright 1982 International Review of Food & Wine Associates.

The Ice Box English Tea Muffin recipe on page 36 is adapted from *Food Editors' Favorites*, published by Hammond Incorporated, Maplewood, New Jersey, and is used by permission.

Introduction

When I was growing up in England, muffins were, for the most part, a romantic treat of the Victorian past. During their heyday, they were usually made in bakeries, carried home, and toasted in front of an open fire (speared on a long toasting fork). They were buttered lavishly and served under a silver dome at all proper breakfasts and teas. I knew what they were supposed to be like: round, flat, yeasty, and craggy on the inside.

Imagine my surprise, then, as a young adult 3,000 miles from the land of muffins, on a sunny Long Island porch, when I was served a basketful of what appeared to be warm, delectable, golden cupcakes but were introduced to me as *muffins*. I naïvely assumed a mistake had been made. I soon learned otherwise. And those first, delicious, baking powder muffins were only a beginning in my education about one of the most comforting of American foods.

Since then, I've enjoyed muffins all over this country: fat ones bursting with blueberries on a wild blueberry farm in Maine; honey bran sunflower seed muffins served with spicy sausage and ranch-produced honey in the North Dakota countryside; corn muffins with country ham and a mess of greens in Richmond, Virginia; cranberry sour cream muffins in Oregon; and raspberry almond muffins in a Carmel, California, bed-and-breakfast inn.

In my own home, I've found that a basket of fragrant muffins always pleases both family and friends, and that the cook gets far more credit than the effort might seem to deserve.

I've also found that American cooks are as inventive with muffins as they are with many other kinds of food. Almost any flavor can be translated into a muffin: corn and jalapeño; Italian sausage; Cheddar cheese and mustard; chocolate and orange (one of my personal favorites).

Muffins are so versatile that they can be enjoyed at any time of day and can serve any mood. I've divided the book into five major sections: breakfast, tea, savory lunch or dinner, English muffins, and special diet. The last section has recipes for spreads and preserves that complement muffins.

Breakfast muffins use various types of flour and grain: whole wheat, triticale, corn meal, oats, buckwheat, bran, and of course white flour. The muffins in this section are the most healthful and nutritious. Served with yogurt and fruit or a wedge of soft cheese, they make breakfast a special occasion. There are recipes for the classics, such as blueberry, bran, and corn, but some are a bit more exotic, like Oregon hazelnut and fig, and whole-wheat applesauce date muffins.

Tea muffins tend to be sweeter. They are best at midmorning or late afternoon, but can really be served at any time. The lemon and ginger muffins, for example, have an exceptionally fresh lemon taste and are wonderful to serve with either hot tea or iced tea on a lazy afternoon. The pumpkin chocolate chip muffins are a delicious snack that children love with a glass of cold milk.

Savory lunch and dinner muffins are packed with interesting flavors, and when served with a big bowl of soup and a salad, they make a complete meal. Whether your choice is muffins Boursin, Cheddar cheese and mustard muffins (great with beer), or sour cream jalapeño corn muffins (for your next barbecue), you will soon be convinced that muffins are no longer just a breakfast food.

Without *English muffins,* which have an entirely different taste and texture, no book on muffins would be complete.

English muffins are made from a thick yeast batter that can be beaten by hand or machine and that requires two short risings. The muffins take about 20 minutes to cook, and you must adjust the heat so they bake slowly without scorching; after that, you don't have to hover over them. Of course, yeast muffins do take longer to make than baking powder muffins, but the results are worth the effort.

If you're on a special diet or have a child, spouse, or friend who is, you probably already know how much people on special diets crave baked goods with old, familiar tastes and textures that also meet their dietary needs. The *special-diet muffins* are quite varied and taste very close to the real thing. Inevitably, some textures will be different. Included are recipes for muffins that are low in sodium, cholesterol, or calories, and free of milk, wheat, or eggs.

Check all ingredients carefully when you are cooking for a person on a special diet. Someone allergic to corn, for example, will also be allergic to cornstarch, corn syrup, and cornstarch-based baking powders. A person on a wheat-free diet may be able to eat oats, rye, buckwheat, and barley grains that contain only a small amount of gluten. But those grains cannot be tolerated by a person on a gluten-free diet, leaving you with only rice, corn, and potato flours with which to cook. In spite of all these caveats, one or more of the recipes in this section should make your special dieter very happy.

Spreads and preserves will make your homemade muffins extra special. The recipes in this section are very quick to prepare. They range from strawberry rhubarb preserves to honey and herb butters as well as a lemon spread that doubles as a cake filling.

MUFFIN BASICS

There are two types of muffins: stirred and creamed. *Stirred muffins* are the simplest muffins of all. The main point to remember is not to overmix the batter. If your muffins have peaked domes and are full of long tunnels with a texture that is on the tough side, you should mix the batter slightly less next time. Stirred muffins are prepared first by thoroughly mixing the dry ingredients with a spoon. It is important that the baking soda and baking powder be evenly distributed; otherwise, the baked muffins will have yellowish holes and an acid flavor. The wet ingredients (egg, milk, melted butter, and so on) are usually whisked together in a separate bowl, then folded into the dry ingredients with a rubber spatula. To fold, you should cut through the center of the mixture with the spatula, turning it slightly up as you turn the bowl, approaching the side of the bowl nearest you. Continue cutting and turning (occasionally you may scrape the sides) until the dry ingredients are moistened. A few lumps will be fine. But keep an eye on the batter; the art of making light, tender muffins is to recognize just when the ingredients are mixed enough. Muffin batters vary from thick to thin, according to the types and amounts of flours and liquids used.

Creamed muffins are richer and taste more like cupcakes than stirred muffins. They have more fat and sugar and a more crumbly, cakelike texture. If the recipe calls for beating soft butter and sugar and then beating in the eggs, you know it is a creamed muffin. The amount of mixing is not quite so crucial with a creamed muffin as it is with a stirred batter, but be sure to fold and not beat when indicated.

When you scoop the batter into the muffin cups, you will find that using a ¼-cup measure is less messy than a spoon and easier to handle in determining equal amounts of batter for each cup. If you're used to spooning, give the scooping method a try and you'll quickly see how much time you save.

All the recipes can be prepared by hand; but because more and more people seem to prefer using a food processor, I've included some recipes that are written for both the food processor and hand method. The food processor eliminates tedious chopping and grating, but both methods produce equally delicious results.

Baking powder and/or baking soda are used to make the muffins rise and to give them their light texture. These ingredients are almost always mixed with the flour to make sure they are evenly dispersed throughout the finished batter. If either the baking powder or baking soda appears to be slightly lumpy when you measure it, put it into a small strainer and sift it into the flour.

When mixed with liquid, baking powder and baking soda give off carbon dioxide, which forms bubbles throughout the batter. When the batter is baked, the flour and egg proteins set around the bubbles, creating the desired light texture. Baking soda is pure sodium bicarbonate, and baking powder contains it. Sodium bicarbonate leaves an alkaline flavor after baking, so it is usually used in combination with an acid ingredient. Baking powder already contains a neutralizing acid. Acid ingredients include such obvious ones as buttermilk, yogurt, sour cream, and citrus juices, and such less obvious ones as apricots, cranberries, apples, molasses, and brown sugar (which contains molasses).

When a recipe calls for yogurt or buttermilk, dried buttermilk powder may be used instead. Dried, cultured buttermilk powder is very convenient to use and is available in most supermarkets, usually near the canned or powdered dried milk section. You can also look in the baking section alongside flour and sugar. Another simple substitute for buttermilk or yogurt is homemade sour milk. To prepare it, put 1 tablespoon of lemon juice or distilled white vinegar into a 1-cup liquid measure and fill it to the 1-cup mark with fresh milk.

Because I prefer the flavor, most of the recipes in this book call for butter. You may, of course, use margarine instead. You may even use vegetable oil (such as corn or safflower), except in recipes in which the butter must be beaten with sugar until pale and fluffy. Also, vegetable oil tends to give some muffins a slightly oily texture.

Muffin recipes are remarkably tolerant, which in recipe-testing lingo means that they can stand about 10 percent too much or too little of any ingredient. Still, for best results, measure ingredients accurately. When you measure the ingredients, don't pack the flour, baking powder, or baking soda; do pack the brown sugar and be sure to level off the excess. Remember that whole-wheat flour and white flour are different and can't be substituted for each other.

Muffins bake best when they are put in a hot oven. You know your own oven; allow time for it to heat properly. Since many oven thermostats are off by 25 degrees or more, it's a sound idea to keep an oven thermometer inside your oven and to check it often. Check the position of racks before you turn on the oven. Muffins bake best in the middle of the oven, not close to either the top or bottom.

I've baked muffins in just about every available type of pan, and I've found surprisingly little difference in the results, whatever the price. Iron, steel, aluminum, and nonstick pans all bake well. If you are about to invest in muffin pans, give serious consideration to ones with a nonstick finish. They are easy to grease, produce muffins that fall right out of the pan, and are a snap to clean. Take care not to scratch the finish by cutting food in the pans or gouging food out of them with a sharp object.

Muffin pans come in two distinct sizes: miniature (about 2 inches across the top and 1 inch deep) and regular. Regular pans vary considerably from one manufacturer to another, and individual cups hold anywhere from 2 to 4 fluid ounces (¼ to ½ cup). It makes little difference which size you use, but do fill the cups about three quarters full. Some recipes may make more or less than a dozen. If less, you may want to fill the empty cups with a small amount of water to keep the heat evenly distributed throughout the pan. If more, you may want to use foil baking cups on a sheet, if the recipe allows. According to the size of the pan and the amount of batter for each cup, you may need to adjust the baking time slightly. For most recipes, you can line the metal muffin cups with foil or paper baking cups instead of greasing the pan. Baking cups, either paper or foil (which can be placed directly on a baking sheet), work especially well for "filled" muffins because fillings such as the marmalade muffins tend to burst out and stick to the muffin cups, making muffins hard to remove.

All muffin pans, even those with a nonstick finish, require greasing. In my opinion the easiest way to grease the cups is with cookware spray, which takes only a few seconds. You can also dip a piece of paper towel in oil or vegetable shortening and rub a thin film of grease around the inside of each muffin cup. Or, when you melt butter for the recipe, add a little extra and brush it inside each muffin cup. With care, muffin pans should last forever, and with frequent use they will develop a well-seasoned, slick surface that will enable the baked muffins to slide out easily. Use a damp cloth or paper towel to wipe out pans that have a nonstick finish; no washing is needed. A nylon scrubber is good for pans that have a stubborn residue. After baking, if muffins don't drop easily from the pan, let them sit for 3 or 4 minutes. Steam will condense around the muffins and help loosen them. If they still don't fall out, loosen them with the rounded tip of a knife.

In the recipes in this book, ranges in baking time are given to allow for differences in ovens, baking pans, the amount of batter put in each cup, and so on. If a recipe says the batter can be used for both regular and miniature muffins, and the baking time is given in a 15- to 25-minute range, take a first peek at 15 minutes. Miniatures could be done; regular muffins will almost certainly need longer. When a muffin is cooked the center will feel springy; your finger should not sink into soft, uncooked batter. You may also test the center of the muffin with a toothpick. When inserted in the middle, it should come out clean, that is, with no uncooked batter sticking to it.

MAKING MUFFINS AHEAD

Almost all baked muffins freeze well for up to three months. Freeze them in a tightly closed plastic bag when they are cool but still fresh. To reheat, place the frozen muffins on a baking sheet in an oven or toaster oven at 350° F. Bake 5 to 10 minutes, until hot.

If you want to freeze muffins ahead for a party, there's an even better way than freezing them baked. *Freeze the unbaked batter.* San Francisco food consultant Charlotte Walker told me about this method, which she discovered while working on her book *Freezing and Drying*. Here's what you do: Line muffin cups with foil or, if the recipe says so, paper baking cups. Fill the cups with the muffin batter and pop the pans in the freezer. When the muffins are frozen hard, transfer them to a plastic bag or freezer container; note the baking temperature on the bag so you don't have to hunt up the recipe again later. When you are ready to bake them, put the frozen muffins back in the muffin cups and place them in a preheated oven. You need to increase the baking time by only 5 or 6 minutes. You can bake all the muffins at once or one or two at a time in a toaster oven. This is a great way to have freshly baked muffins every day for breakfast, but don't try it with any special diet muffins.

There's one more technique you can use if you want to serve hot, freshly baked muffins with a meal but have little time to cook just before mealtime. Measure and mix the dry ingredients an hour or even a day ahead. Get out the pans and grease them (with cookware spray) just before baking. Mix the wet ingredients; they can be left at room temperature for a couple of hours or refrigerated for a longer period. (Add melted butter just before baking.) When you are ready to eat, turn on the oven and just before you think it is hot enough, mix up the batter and fill the pans.

QUICK CHECK

1. When a recipe does not say you may use foil or paper baking cups, they don't work well for that particular batter.

2. The fastest and easiest way to grease muffin pans is with a vegetable cookware spray.

3. Allow time for the oven to heat. It can heat as you prepare the batter.

4. You can assemble and mix the dry ingredients and the wet ingredients separately, ahead of time. But once the batter is mixed, get the muffins in the oven promptly, unless the instructions state otherwise.

BREAKFAST MUFFINS

THE BEST BLUEBERRY MUFFINS

Bursting with berries, these are the best blueberry muffins of all. The secret is an extra half cup of blueberries, which are mashed and then added to the batter. *Serve warm, with Honey Butter (page 84).*

- ½ cup (l stick) butter, at room temperature
- 1 cup granulated sugar, or slightly less depending on tartness of blueberries
- 2 large eggs
- 1 teaspoon vanilla extract
- 2 teaspoons baking powder
- ¼ teaspoon salt
- 2½ cups blueberries (mash ½ cup with a fork)
- 2 cups all-purpose flour
- ½ cup milk
- 1 tablespoon sugar mixed with ¼ teaspoon ground nutmeg

Heat oven to 375° F. Grease 12 regular muffin cups, including the area between each cup, or use foil baking cups.

In a medium-size bowl, beat butter until creamy. Beat in the sugar until pale and fluffy. Beat in eggs, one at a time. Beat in vanilla, baking powder, and salt.

Mix mashed berries into batter.

Fold in half the flour with a spatula, then half the milk. Add remaining flour and milk. Fold in remaining blueberries.

Scoop batter into muffin cups. Sprinkle with nutmeg sugar.

Bake 25 to 30 minutes, or until golden brown. Let muffins cool at least 30 minutes in the pan before removing.

THE BEST BRAN MUFFINS

For some people, freshly brewed coffee and a hearty bran muffin are the only way to start the day. I find that the kind most often found in coffee shops is dry and too sweet; "health food" muffins are too heavy. These are light and delicate, just what bran muffins should be. With scrambled eggs and crisp bacon, heaven! Bran muffins are excellent topped with Honey Butter (page 84), Very Strawberry Butter (page 85), preserves, or Lemon Spread (page 86). *Serve warm or at room temperature.*

> 2 *large eggs*
> ¼ *cup packed light brown sugar*
> 1 *cup milk*
> ¼ *cup vegetable oil*
> 1½ *cups wheat bran cereal*
> ½ *cup oat bran (see note)*
> ½ *cup all-purpose flour*
> 2 *teaspoons baking powder*

Heat oven to 375° F. Grease muffin cups, or use paper or foil baking cups.

Beat eggs and brown sugar in a medium-size bowl until smooth. Whisk in milk and oil. Stir in wheat bran cereal. Let soak 10 minutes (longer, if more convenient).

Thoroughly mix oat bran, all-purpose flour, and baking powder in a large bowl.

Add soaked bran mixture and fold in with a rubber spatula just until dry ingredients are moistened.

Scoop batter into muffin cups. Bake 20 to 25 minutes, or until brown and firm in the center. Turn out onto a rack to cool.

NOTE: Oat bran can be found in the cereal or health food sections of most grocery stores.

VARIATIONS: Brush muffins with 2 or 3 tablespoons of maple syrup as soon as they are removed from the oven.

Add ½ cup raisins or ½ cup walnuts to batter.

BANANA BRAN MUFFINS

Topped with Honey Butter (page 84) or Quick Apricot Preserves (page 88), these moist muffins are perfect for breakfast. *Serve warm.*

    1 large egg
    ¾ cup packed light brown sugar
    1⅓ cups mashed ripe bananas
    ½ cup raisins or walnuts
    ⅓ cup vegetable oil
    1 teaspoon vanilla extract
    ¾ cup all-purpose flour
    ¾ cup whole-wheat flour
    ½ cup oat bran or unprocessed wheat
       bran (miller's bran)
    2 teaspoons baking powder
    ½ teaspoon baking soda
    1 teaspoon ground cinnamon
    ¼ teaspoon salt

Heat oven to 375° F. Grease muffin cups, or use foil or paper baking cups.

Beat egg and sugar in a medium-size bowl. When smooth, beat in bananas, raisins, oil, and vanilla. Let stand a minute.

Thoroughly mix flours, bran, baking powder, baking soda, cinnamon, and salt in a large bowl. Add banana mixture and fold in with a spatula just until dry ingredients are moistened.

Scoop batter into muffin cups. Bake 15 to 25 minutes, or until brown and springy to the touch in the center. Turn out onto a rack to cool.

HONEY BRAN MUFFINS

Make these with unprocessed wheat bran—not bran flakes or shreds sold as breakfast cereal. Honey adds flavor and moisture; you can experiment with different kinds such as orange blossom or sage. *Serve warm.*

1¼ cups unprocessed wheat bran
   (miller's bran)
1¼ cups all-purpose flour
  2 teaspoons baking powder
  ¼ teaspoon salt
  1 cup milk
  ¼ cup honey
  1 large egg
  4 tablespoons butter, melted

Heat oven to 375° F. Grease muffin cups, or use foil baking cups.

Thoroughly mix bran, flour, baking powder, and salt in a large bowl.

Put milk, honey, and egg in a small bowl; beat with a fork or whisk until well blended. Whisk in butter. Pour over dry ingredients and fold or stir in with a rubber spatula until dry ingredients are moistened.

Scoop the batter into the muffin cups. Bake 18 to 24 minutes, or until lightly browned and firm and springy to the touch in the center. Remove from pans and let cool a few minutes before serving.

VARIATION: Add ½ cup chopped walnuts, or raisins to batter.

REFRIGERATOR BRAN MUFFINS

28 REGULAR MUFFINS

Here's a recipe that breaks all the rules about baking muffins as soon as the batter is mixed. This batter can be stored in the refrigerator for up to six weeks and baked as needed! With a batch of it in your refrigerator, you can enjoy the luxury of fresh-baked muffins every morning. For baking just a few, a toaster oven works fine. *Serve hot.*

> 2 *large eggs*
> 1 *cup granulated sugar*
> ½ *cup butter, very soft or melted*
> 1 *cup black coffee or water*
> 2 *cups buttermilk* or *6 tablespoons dried buttermilk and 2 cups water*
> 2½ *cups all-purpose flour*
> 2½ *teaspoons baking soda*
> 3 *cups wheat bran cereal*

Put eggs, sugar, and butter in a large bowl; whisk with a wire whisk to mix. Whisk in liquids; mixture will look curdled. Add flour and baking soda. Whisk until just mixed. Stir or fold in bran.

Scrape batter into a refrigerator container. Cover and refrigerate. (If you want to bake batter without storing, let it stand 15 to 20 minutes for bran to soften.)

To bake: heat oven to 375° F. Grease muffin cups or use foil baking cups. Stir batter gently to mix. Scoop ¼ cup into each muffin cup. Bake about 20 minutes, or until springy to the touch in the center. Let cool 5 minutes before serving.

WALNUT DATE MUFFINS

These muffins are wonderful for breakfast with fruit and yogurt or a scoop of cottage cheese. *Serve warm.*

1 cup wheat bran cereal
¾ cup milk
1 large egg
¼ cup vegetable oil
½ cup chopped dates
½ cup chopped walnuts or pecans
1 cup all-purpose flour
¼ cup granulated sugar
2½ teaspoons baking powder

Mix cereal with milk in a medium-size bowl; let stand 3 to 5 minutes until milk has been absorbed.

Heat oven to 400° F; grease muffin cups or use foil baking cups.

Beat egg and oil into soaked cereal. Stir in the chopped dates and walnuts.

Thoroughly mix flour, sugar, and baking powder in a large bowl. Pour in liquid ingredients. Fold in with a rubber spatula, just until dry ingredients are moistened.

Scoop batter into muffin cups. Bake 15 to 25 minutes, or until springy to the touch in the center. Turn out onto a rack to cool thoroughly. Wrap in a plastic bag (or put in an airtight container) and let stand several hours for flavor to develop. Reheat before serving.

WHOLE-WHEAT APPLESAUCE DATE MUFFINS

Good breakfast or snack muffins topped with apple butter, or Very Strawberry Butter (page 85). These should be made a day ahead so the flavors can develop and mellow. *Serve at room temperature.*

  2 *cups whole-wheat flour*
  2 *teaspoons baking powder*
  1 *teaspoon ground cinnamon*
 ¼ *teaspoon salt*
  2 *large eggs*
 ¼ *cup packed dark brown sugar*
1½ *cups unsweetened applesauce*
 ¼ *cup vegetable oil*
 ½ *cup chopped dates*

Heat oven to 375° F. Grease muffin cups or use foil baking cups.

Thoroughly mix flour, baking powder, cinnamon, and salt in a large bowl.

Break eggs into another bowl. Add brown sugar and beat until smooth. Add applesauce and oil. Whisk until well blended. Stir in dates. Pour over dry ingredients and fold in just until dry ingredients are moistened.

Scoop batter into muffin cups. Bake 20 to 25 minutes, or until brown and springy to the touch in the center. Turn out on a rack to cool. Place in a plastic bag and store until the next day.

BROWN SUGAR OATMEAL MUFFINS

12 REGULAR MUFFINS

Oatmeal is a good source of fiber. For a change from oatmeal cereal, these muffins are great with Very Strawberry Butter (page 85) or Quick Rhubarb Strawberry Preserves (page 87). *Serve warm.*

  1 cup old-fashioned oats
  1 cup whole-wheat flour
  ½ cup all-purpose flour
  2 teaspoons baking powder
  ½ teaspoon salt
  2 large eggs
  ¾ cup packed dark brown sugar
  ¾ cup milk
  ¼ cup (½ stick) butter, melted; or
       vegetable oil
  1 teaspoon vanilla extract

Heat oven to 400° F. Grease muffin cups, or use foil or paper baking cups.

Thoroughly mix oats, flours, baking powder, and salt in a large bowl.

Whisk eggs and brown sugar in another bowl. When smooth, whisk in milk, melted butter, and vanilla. Pour over dry ingredients. Fold in with a rubber spatula, just until dry ingredients are moistened.

Scoop the batter into muffin cups. Bake 15 to 25 minutes, or until springy to the touch in the center. Turn out onto a rack to cool.

MARMALADE MUFFINS

This is a perfect breakfast muffin—light and delicate, with a tangy filling. Be sure to use a flavorful, good-quality marmalade. If the marmalade is very sweet, decrease the sugar to 2 tablespoons. *Serve hot or warm.*

2 cups all-purpose flour
1/4 cup granulated sugar
1 tablespoon baking powder
1/4 teaspoon salt
1 large egg
1 cup plain yogurt or buttermilk
1/4 cup (1/2 stick) butter, melted
1 teaspoon vanilla extract
1/4 cup orange, grapefruit, or ginger marmalade

Heat oven to 375° F. Grease 8 regular muffin cups or use foil baking cups.

Thoroughly mix flour, sugar, baking powder, and salt in a large bowl.

In a medium-size bowl, whisk egg with yogurt, butter, and vanilla until smooth. Pour over flour mixture and fold in just until dry ingredients are moistened.

Spoon 1 heaping tablespoon of batter into each of the muffin cups. Press back of spoon softly on batter to make a small well. Fill with about 1 teaspoon of marmalade. Top with approximately 2 more tablespoons batter (enough to cover marmalade).

Bake 25 to 30 minutes, or until golden brown. Let cool about 5 minutes before removing from pans.

FOUR-GRAIN MUFFINS

12 REGULAR

Perfect all-around muffins that, when made with a larger quantity of sugar, are delicious for breakfast served with Quick Apricot Preserves (page 88). When prepared with less sugar, they are superb with salads, quiches, and casseroles. *Serve warm.*

½ cup triticale flour
½ cup buckwheat flour
½ cup all-purpose flour
½ cup oat bran (see note, page 13)
2 to 4 tablespoons granulated sugar
1 tablespoon baking powder
¼ teaspoon salt
1 large egg
1 cup milk
4 tablespoons (½ stick) butter, melted; or vegetable oil

Heat oven to 375° F. Grease muffin cups, or use foil or paper baking cups.

Thoroughly mix flours, bran, sugar, baking powder, and salt in a large bowl.

Whisk egg in a small bowl. Whisk in milk and butter. Pour over dry ingredients. Fold in with a rubber spatula, just until dry ingredients are moistened.

Scoop batter into muffin cups. Bake 20 to 25 minutes, or until light brown and firm to the touch in the center.

Turn out onto a rack and cool at least 15 minutes before serving.

MAPLE CINNAMON BROWN RICE MUFFINS

12 REGULAR OR 24 MINIATURE MUFFINS

Moist, and flavored with maple and currants, these muffins are comforting for breakfast. They are especially good in miniature size. The rice adds flavor and texture. *Serve hot or warm.*

1¼ cups whole-wheat flour
  2 teaspoons baking powder
  1 teaspoon ground cinnamon
  ¼ teaspoon salt
  2 large eggs
  ⅓ cup cream, evaporated milk or milk
  ⅓ cup maple syrup
  1 cup cooked brown rice (cool before using)
  ½ cup currants or raisins; or prunes
     snipped into small pieces
  3 tablespoons butter, melted; or vegetable oil

Heat oven to 375° F. Grease muffin cups, or use foil or paper baking cups.

Thoroughly mix flour, baking powder, cinnamon, and salt in a large bowl.

Whisk eggs in another bowl; whisk in cream and maple syrup. Stir in rice, currants, and butter.

Pour egg mixture over dry ingredients. Fold in with a rubber spatula, just until dry ingredients are moistened.

Scoop the batter into muffin cups. Bake 20 to 25 minutes, or until no longer damp in the center. Let cool 5 minutes before turning out onto a rack.

YANKEE MAPLE CORN MUFFINS

Unlike most corn breads favored in the South, these muffins are on the sweet side. The maple syrup adds a delightful flavor. Try them with Honey Butter (page 84) or preserves, accompanied by orange spice tea or freshly brewed coffee. *Serve warm.*

2   cups all-purpose flour
1   cup yellow corn meal
1   tablespoon baking powder
¾   teaspoon salt
2   large eggs
¼   cup packed light brown sugar
1   cup milk
¼   to ⅓ cup maple syrup
6   tablespoons (¾ stick) butter, melted

Heat oven to 350° F. Grease muffin cups or use foil baking cups.

Thoroughly mix flour, corn meal, baking powder, and salt in a large bowl.

Whisk eggs and brown sugar in another bowl until smooth. Add milk and maple syrup and whisk to mix. Pour over dry ingredients and add 4 tablespoons of the melted butter. Fold in with a rubber spatula just until dry ingredients are moistened.

Scoop batter into prepared cups. Bake 25 to 30 minutes, or until golden brown and firm in the center. Let cool in pan 5 minutes. Brush tops with remaining melted butter.

OREGON HAZELNUT AND
FIG MUFFINS

Firm-textured muffins with the rich, toasty flavor of hazelnuts, these are excellent for breakfast with a wedge of Cheddar, Havarti, or Monterey Jack cheese. The nuts can be prepared several days before you use them; store in an airtight jar. *Serve at room temperature.*

½ cup hazelnuts (also called filberts)
1½ cups all-purpose flour
½ cup oat bran (see note, page 13)
1 tablespoon baking powder
¼ teaspoon salt
4 ounces black Mission or other
  dried figs (½ cup or about 8 large
  figs), tough stems snipped off
1 cup milk
2 large eggs
¼ cup packed light brown sugar
4 tablespoons (½ stick) butter

Heat oven to 375° F. Put hazelnuts in a pie pan or other metal baking pan with sides so nuts won't roll off. Bake 10 to 15 minutes until skins split and nuts turn pale brown. (You can toast the nuts in a toaster oven while your regular oven heats.) Pour toasted nuts onto a clean dish towel, wrap the towel around the nuts, and rub them to loosen skins. Uncover nuts and let cool about 5 minutes.

While nuts are toasting, grease muffin cups and measure

remaining ingredients. Mix flour, bran, baking powder, and salt in a large bowl.

Pick out nuts (don't worry if some of the skins remain) and grind them a few at a time in a blender. Add to flour mixture and stir to mix.

Cut up figs; purée with milk, eggs, and brown sugar in blender until figs are in small pieces. Melt butter; pour into blender and process briefly to blend.

Pour fig mixture over dry ingredients. Fold in with a rubber spatula just until dry ingredients are moistened.

Scoop batter into muffin cups. Bake 20 to 25 minutes, or until muffins are firm and springy to the touch. Turn out onto a rack and let cool for at least 1 hour for flavor to develop.

NOTE: If you have a food processor, put skinned nuts, flour, baking powder, and salt in work bowl; process until nuts are finely ground. Add bran and cut-up cold butter and process a few seconds, using on/off lever, until butter is incorporated. Tip mixture into a large bowl. Put figs, eggs, brown sugar, and milk in processor. Process until figs are finely chopped. Pour over flour mixture and continue as above.

TEA MUFFINS

CRANBERRY ALMOND
SOUR CREAM MUFFINS

8 REGULAR MUFFINS

This is a perfect muffin for tea time served in place of coffee cake. *Serve warm.*

1½ cups all-purpose flour
½ cup granulated sugar
1 teaspoon baking powder
¼ teaspoon baking soda
¼ teaspoon salt
2 large eggs
¼ cup (½ stick) butter, melted
½ cup sour cream
½ teaspoon almond extract
¾ cup sliced unblanched almonds
½ cup whole-berry cranberry sauce

Heat oven to 375° F. Line muffin pans with foil baking cups, or place baking cups on a baking sheet.

Mix flour, sugar, baking powder, baking soda, and salt in a large bowl.

Break eggs into another bowl. Whisk in butter, sour cream, and almond extract. When blended, stir in ½ cup almonds.

Pour egg mixture over dry ingredients and fold in just until dry ingredients are moistened.

Spoon 2 scant tablespoons of batter into each baking cup. Top with a level tablespoon of cranberry sauce, then with remaining batter. Sprinkle with remaining almonds.

Bake 30 to 35 minutes, or until brown and springy to the touch. Let stand 20 minutes before removing muffins from cups.

APPLE STREUSEL MUFFINS

The delicious crumb topping makes these muffins taste like miniature coffee cakes. Good at tea time and also for brunch. *Cool at least 1 hour before serving.*

TOPPING

- ½ cup chopped walnuts
- ¼ cup all-purpose flour
- 3 tablespoons granulated sugar
- 2 tablespoons butter, at room temperature
- ¼ teaspoon ground cinnamon

BATTER

- 1½ cups all-purpose flour
- ½ cup granulated sugar
- 2 teaspoons baking powder
- 1 teaspoon ground cinnamon
- ¼ teaspoon ground allspice
- ¼ teaspoon baking soda
- ¼ teaspoon salt
- 2 large eggs
- 1 cup sour cream
- ¼ cup (½ stick) butter, melted
- 1 cup diced unpeeled apple, preferably a tart apple such as Granny Smith or Greenings

Heat oven to 375° F. Grease muffin cups or use foil baking cups.

Put streusel topping ingredients into a medium-size bowl. Mix with a fork, then crumble with fingers until mixture looks like chopped walnuts.

To make the muffin batter, thoroughly mix flour, sugar, baking powder, cinnamon, allspice, baking soda, and salt in a large bowl.

Break eggs into another bowl. Add sour cream and melted butter, and whisk until well blended. Stir in diced apple.

Pour egg mixture over flour mixture and fold in just until dry ingredients are moistened.

Scoop batter into muffin cups. Top each muffin with about 2 teaspoons of the streusel topping.

Bake 20 to 25 minutes, or until browned. A toothpick inserted into the center should come out clean. Remove from pans and let cool at least 1 hour before serving.

FRESH LEMON AND GINGER MUFFINS

12 REGULAR OR 48 MINIATURE MUFFINS

Bursting with bright, fresh lemon flavor and just a hint of ginger, these muffins are wonderful with either hot or iced tea or with a long drink on a lazy afternoon. Their special fresh flavor comes from a lemon sugar dip. They are especially good in the miniature size. Using the speedy food processor method (below) eliminates grating the lemon peel. *Serve hot or warm.*

 2 *tablespoons coarsely chopped, peeled fresh ginger root*
 1 *or 2 lemons, well scrubbed and patted dry*
½ *cup (1 stick) butter, at room temperature*
 1 *cup granulated sugar*
 2 *large eggs*
 1 *teaspoon baking soda*
 1 *cup plain yogurt or buttermilk*
 2 *cups all-purpose flour*
¼ *cup freshly squeezed lemon juice*
 2 *tablespoons granulated sugar*

Heat oven to 375° F. Grease muffin cups or use foil or paper baking cups. Finely chop the ginger. Finely grate the lemon peel so you have 2 tablespoons.

In a large bowl, beat butter and the 1 cup sugar with a wooden spoon or electric mixer until pale and fluffy. Beat in eggs, one at a time. Add ginger and lemon peel.

Stir baking soda into yogurt or buttermilk; it will start to bubble and rise up.

Fold flour into ginger mixture one third at a time, alternating with the yogurt. When well blended, scoop into muffin cups. Bake 18 to 20 minutes, or until lightly browned and springy to the touch.

While muffins bake, mix lemon juice and the 2 tablespoons sugar in a small dish. Stir until sugar dissolves.

When muffins are baked, remove from oven and let cool 3 to 5 minutes in pan. Remove from pan and dip top and bottom in the lemon juice and sugar mixture.

NOTE: If you have a food processor use this method: Peel one lemon with a vegetable peeler. Put ginger, lemon peel, and the 1 cup sugar into the food processor, fitted with a steel blade. Process 1 to 2 minutes, scraping sides once, until lemon peel and ginger are very finely chopped. Add butter; process about 30 seconds until creamy. Add eggs, one at a time, processing briefly after each addition. Scrape mixture into a large bowl; if it looks curdled, don't worry. Add baking soda, yogurt, and flour and continue as above.

PECAN ORANGE MUFFINS

This light, flavorful muffin is good with a spicy herb tea and Honey Butter (page 84). Martha Stewart, caterer and cookbook author, serves miniature muffins similar to these with a dab of apple jelly and a slice of smoked turkey. They make an unusual and delicious appetizer. *Serve hot or warm.*

   1 *medium-size eating orange, well*
     scrubbed and wiped dry
 ³⁄₄ *cup pecans*
 ¹⁄₂ *cup (l stick) butter, at room*
     temperature
   1 *cup plus 1 tablespoon granulated*
     sugar
   2 *large eggs*
   1 *teaspoon baking soda*
   2 *cups all-purpose flour*
   1 *cup plain yogurt or buttermilk*
 ¹⁄₃ *cup freshly squeezed orange juice*

Heat oven to 375° F. Grease muffin cups, or use foil or paper baking cups.

Finely grate the orange peel. Try to remove as little white pith as possible. Finely chop pecans.

Beat butter and the 1 cup sugar with an electric mixer until pale and creamy. Beat in eggs, one at a time. Stir in the baking soda and grated peel.

Fold in half the flour, then half the yogurt. Repeat, then fold in pecans.

Scoop batter into muffin cups. Bake 20 to 25 minutes, or until browned.

Remove from oven. Brush or spoon orange juice over hot muffins and sprinkle with the 1 tablespoon sugar. Let stand 5 minutes before removing from pans.

NOTE: If you are using a food processor, remove only the thin orange part of the orange peel with a vegetable peeler. Put peel and the 1 cup sugar in food processor. Process until peel is finely chopped, about 1 minute. Add butter and process until creamy, about 1 minute. Add eggs, one at a time, processing after each addition until well combined. Scrape down sides. Add yogurt and baking soda and process to mix, scraping down sides once more. Sprinkle pecans, then flour, over butter mixture. Press on/off lever three or four times, just until flour is incorporated and pecans are finely chopped. Continue as above.

PUMPKIN CHOCOLATE CHIP MUFFINS

12 REGULAR OR 48 MINIATURE MUFFINS

Incredibly rich and spicy, filled with chocolate chips and crunchy almonds, these muffins are delicious with steaming cups of espresso. Children also love them with cold milk. *Make one or two days ahead for best flavor.*

½ cup (1¼ ounces) sliced unblanched almonds

1⅔ cups all-purpose flour

1 cup granulated sugar

1 tablespoon pumpkin pie spice

1 teaspoon baking soda

¼ teaspoon baking powder

¼ teaspoon salt

2 large eggs

1 cup plain pumpkin (half of a 1-pound can)

½ cup (l stick) butter, melted

1 cup (6 ounces) chocolate chips

Heat oven to 350° F. Put almonds on a baking sheet or pie pan and bake about 5 minutes, just until lightly browned; watch carefully so almonds don't burn. (You can also toast them in a toaster oven.) Slide almonds off the baking sheet so they cool quickly.

Grease muffin cups, or use foil or paper baking cups.

Thoroughly mix flour, sugar, pie spice, baking soda, baking powder, and salt in a large bowl.

Break eggs into another bowl. Add pumpkin and butter, and whisk until well blended. Stir in chocolate chips and almonds. Pour over dry ingredients and fold in with a rubber spatula just until dry ingredients are moistened.

Scoop batter evenly into muffin cups. Bake 20 to 25 minutes, or until puffed and springy to the touch in the center. Turn out onto a rack to cool. Wrap in a plastic bag and keep for 1 or 2 days. Reheat before serving.

DONNA MORGAN'S ICE BOX ENGLISH TEA MUFFINS

12 REGULAR MUFFINS

A treasured old family recipe from the food editor of the *Salt Lake Tribune*, this is one of my favorites. The muffins are perfect for a special tea or coffee party—or even a wedding reception. The batter can be baked right away or refrigerated for up to 2 weeks before baking. *Serve warm or at room temperature.*

BATTER

- 2 cups all-purpose flour
- 2 teaspoons baking powder
- ½ teaspoon salt
- ¼ teaspoon ground cinnamon
- ¾ cup granulated sugar
- ½ cup (1 stick) butter, at room temperature
- 1 large egg
- 1 cup milk
- ¾ cup raisins

TOPPING

- ½ cup packed light brown sugar
- ¼ cup chopped pecans
- 1 teaspoon ground cinnamon

Heat oven to 350° F. Grease muffin cups, or use foil or paper baking cups.

Mix flour, baking powder, salt, and cinnamon in a small bowl. Using a wooden spoon or electric mixer, beat sugar and butter in a large bowl. Beat in egg. Add flour mixture to egg mixture about one third at a time, alternating with milk and ending with flour. Stir just until blended. Fold in raisins.

Mix topping ingredients in a small bowl.

Muffins may be baked right away, or batter and topping may be covered tightly in separate containers and refrigerated for up to 2 weeks. Stir before baking.

Scoop batter into muffin cups, using just over ¼ cup for each. Sprinkle with topping. Bake about 20 minutes, or until springy to the touch in the center. Cool 5 minutes before removing from pans.

GOLDEN RAISIN ROSEMARY MUFFINS

12 REGULAR OR 24 MINIATURE MUFFINS

Inspired by the rosemary tea-cake recipe in the *Fanny Farmer Baking Book* by Marion Cunningham, these unique muffins are ready in no time at all. They are particularly delicious as miniatures. *Serve hot.*

¾ cup milk
½ cup golden raisins
 1 teaspoon dried rosemary leaves
¼ cup (½ stick) butter
1½ cups all-purpose flour
½ cup granulated sugar
 2 teaspoons baking powder
¼ teaspoon salt
 1 large egg

Simmer milk, raisins, and rosemary for 2 minutes in a small saucepan. Remove from heat, add butter, and stir until melted. Let cool. (Placing the saucepan in a small bowl of cold water will cool the contents quickly, in 3 or 4 minutes.)

Heat oven to 350° F. Grease muffin cups or use foil baking cups.

Mix flour, sugar, baking powder, and salt in a large bowl.

Whisk egg into milk mixture. Pour over dry ingredients and fold in with a rubber spatula just until dry ingredients are moistened.

Scoop batter into muffin cups. Bake about 20 minutes, or until browned and springy in the center. Turn out of pan and serve hot; or cool on a rack.

SPICY SOUR CREAM RAISIN MUFFINS

12 REGULAR MUFFINS

Dark, rich, and spicy in flavor, these are especially good at holiday time topped with cream cheese or Honey Butter (page 84). They make a special treat late at night with a glass of sherry! *Serve hot.*

  2 *large eggs*
 ½ *cup sour cream*
 ½ *cup milk*
  2 *tablespoons instant coffee granules*
 ¾ *cup raisins*
1½ *cups all-purpose flour*
 ½ *cup plus 1 tablespoon old-fashioned oats*
 ½ *cup granulated sugar*
  2 *teaspoons baking powder*
 ½ *teaspoon each ground cloves, cinnamon, and allspice*

Put eggs, sour cream, milk, and instant coffee into a bowl. Whisk until well blended. Stir in raisins. Let stand about 5 minutes while coffee dissolves. Stir to mix.

While the coffee is dissolving, heat oven to 375° F. and grease the muffin cups or use foil or paper baking cups.

Mix flour, the ½ cup oats, the sugar, baking powder, and spices in a large bowl. Add sour cream mixture and fold in with a rubber spatula just until dry ingredients are moistened.

Scoop batter into muffin cups. Sprinkle with the 1 tablespoon oats. Bake 20 to 23 minutes, or until browned and springy to the touch in the center. Serve immediately.

NUTMEG MUFFINS

12 REGULAR OR 36 MINIATURE MUFFINS

This is a nice, simple muffin you'll make again and again. It's good with prune butter, Honey Butter (page 84), preserves, or Lemon Spread (page 86). *Serve hot or warm.*

2 cups all-purpose flour
3 tablespoons granulated sugar
1 tablespoon baking powder
½ teaspoon freshly grated nutmeg, or
    ¾ to 1 teaspoon ground nutmeg
¼ teaspoon salt
2 large eggs
1 cup milk
¼ cup (½ stick) butter, melted

Heat oven to 375° F. Grease muffin cups, or use foil or paper baking cups.

Thoroughly mix flour, sugar, baking powder, nutmeg, and salt in a large bowl.

Break eggs into another bowl. Whisk in milk and butter until well blended. Pour over dry ingredients and fold in with a rubber spatula, just until dry ingredients are moistened.

Scoop batter into muffin cups. Bake 15 to 20 minutes, or until lightly browned and springy to the touch in the center. Turn out onto a rack.

PEANUT BUTTER AND JELLY MUFFINS

My husband and I once served these muffins with great success to ten small children we invited over for a tea party. But you don't need to stage a party to make these muffins; children love them anytime. *Serve warm or at room temperature.*

2 cups all-purpose flour
3 tablespoons granulated sugar
1 tablespoon baking powder
¾ cup creamy peanut butter
1 large egg
1 cup milk
   About ⅓ cup raspberry or strawberry jelly

Heat oven to 350° F. Grease nonstick muffin cups or use foil baking cups.

Mix flour, sugar, and baking powder in a large bowl. Put peanut butter and egg in another bowl and beat with a wooden spoon until smooth. Add milk a little at a time, stirring after each addition.

Pour peanut butter mixture over dry ingredients and fold in with a rubber spatula just until dry ingredients are moistened. Mixture will be stiff—more like a dough than a batter.

Spoon 2 scant tablespoons batter into each muffin cup and smooth surface out with your fingers until it touches the edge of the baking cup. Top each muffin with a heaping teaspoon of jelly, then cover with 2 more tablespoons batter.

Bake 20 to 25 minutes or until lightly browned.

CHOCOLATE ORANGE MUFFINS

These are fabulous any time, but especially with freshly brewed coffee or espresso.

With the quick and easy food processor method (below) the muffin batter can be prepared in the time it takes the oven to heat up. Use a good-quality eating chocolate such as Lindt or Tobler. *Serve hot or warm.*

2 *medium-size eating oranges, well scrubbed and wiped dry*
3 *ounces bittersweet chocolate*
1 *cup granulated sugar*
½ *cup (1 stick) butter, at room temperature*
2 *large eggs*
½ *cup plain yogurt or buttermilk*
½ *cup freshly squeezed orange juice*
1 *teaspoon baking powder*
½ *teaspoon baking soda*
2 *cups all-purpose flour*

Heat oven to 375° F. Grease muffin cups or use foil baking cups.

Finely grate orange peel. Try to take just the orange part. A little white pith will probably adhere.

Chop chocolate with a large knife.

Using a wooden spoon or an electric mixer, beat sugar and butter in a large bowl until pale and fluffy. Beat in eggs one at a time. Add orange peel.

Add yogurt, orange juice, baking powder, and baking soda.

Mix very well. Batter will be quite liquid.

Sprinkle flour, then chocolate, over batter. Fold gently, just enough to blend in flour.

Scoop the batter into the muffin cups. Bake 15 to 25 minutes, or until golden brown and springy to the touch. Turn out onto a rack.

NOTE: With the food processor method, use the pulse on/off lever of the food processor to chop the chocolate coarsely. Tip out onto a sheet of wax paper. Remove orange peel with a vegetable peeler. Put peel and sugar in food processor and process about 30 seconds until peel is finely chopped. Add butter and process a few seconds until creamy. Scrape sides. Add eggs one at a time, processing after each addition. Add yogurt, orange juice, baking powder, and soda. Process a few seconds to blend. Scrape mixture into a large bowl. Gently fold in flour and chocolate. Continue as above.

PECAN STICKY MUFFINS

Everyone who loves sticky buns adores these, and they are so much easier to make. *Serve warm.*

TOPPING

¼ cup (½ stick) butter, melted
¼ cup packed dark brown sugar
48 pecan halves, or about 1 cup chopped pecans

BATTER

1½ cups all-purpose flour
½ cup oat bran (see note, page 13)
1 tablespoon baking powder
1 teaspoon ground cinnamon
¼ teaspoon salt
2 large eggs
¼ cup packed dark brown sugar
1 cup milk
¼ cup (½ stick) butter, melted
1 teaspoon vanilla extract

Heat oven to 350° F. Use muffin cups with a nonstick finish instead of foil or paper baking cups so that you do not lose the topping.

For the topping, put 1 teaspoon melted butter, 1 teaspoon dark brown sugar, and 4 pecan halves into each muffin cup.

To make the batter, mix flour, oat bran, baking powder,

cinnamon, and salt in a large bowl.

Beat eggs and brown sugar in another bowl. When smooth, whisk in milk, butter, and vanilla.

Pour egg mixture over flour mixture. Fold in with a rubber spatula just until dry ingredients are moistened.

Scoop about ¼ cup batter into each muffin cup. Bake 25 to 30 minutes, or until lightly browned and firm in the center. As soon as you take the muffins from the oven, turn the pan upside down onto a sheet of foil. Let stand 5 minutes, then remove pan. (A little of the sticky mixture will remain in the pan.) Serve muffins warm.

VARIATION:

UPSIDE-DOWN APRICOT GEMS. To make 36 miniature muffins, substitute 36 dried apricot halves for the pecans. Cover the apricots with water in a glass measure or small saucepan. Heat 3 to 4 minutes in a microwave oven to soften, or simmer for 5 minutes on the range. Drain apricots and spread out on a paper towel to dry. Heat oven to 350° F. Grease miniature muffin pans that have a nonstick finish. Put about ¼ teaspoon melted butter in each muffin cup, add a good sprinkle of brown sugar, and top with an apricot half. Prepare batter as for pecan sticky muffins; spoon about 1 tablespoon over each apricot. Tap pan lightly on counter to settle batter. Bake 20 to 25 minutes, or until lightly browned. Immediately turn pan upside down on a plate or sheet of foil. Let stand 3 to 5 minutes, then remove pan.

DARK CARROT RAISIN NUT MUFFINS

These richly colored muffins remind me of hermit cookies. They are delicious plain or with Honey Butter (page 84). For a miniature, emergency birthday cake, frost with a cream cheese frosting. *Serve hot or warm.*

1 cup all-purpose flour
½ cup whole-wheat flour
1 tablespoon baking powder
½ teaspoon ground cinnamon
¼ teaspoon salt
2 large eggs
½ cup packed dark or light brown sugar
¾ cup milk
¼ cup (½ stick) butter, melted; or vegetable oil
1 cup coarsely grated carrots
½ cup raisins
½ cup coarsely chopped walnuts or sunflower seeds

Heat oven to 375° F. Grease muffin cups, or use foil or paper baking cups.

Mix flours, baking powder, cinnamon, and salt in a large bowl.

Whisk eggs and brown sugar in another bowl. When smooth, whisk in milk and butter. Stir in carrots, raisins, and nuts or sunflower seeds. Pour over flour mixture and fold in with a rubber spatula just until dry ingredients are moistened.

Scoop batter into muffin cups. Bake 20 to 25 minutes, or until springy to the touch in the center. Turn out onto a rack.

RASPBERRY ALMOND MUFFINS

16 REGULAR MUFFINS

The raspberry preserves and almond paste tucked inside these delicate muffins make them a surprising treat. *Serve warm.*

About 5 ounces almond paste
½ *cup (1 stick) butter, at room temperature*
¾ *cup granulated sugar*
2 *large eggs*
1 *teaspoon baking powder*
½ *teaspoon baking soda*
1 *teaspoon almond extract*
2 *cups all-purpose flour*
1 *cup plain yogurt or buttermilk*
About ¼ cup raspberry preserves

Heat oven to 350° F. Line muffin pans with foil baking cups.

Cut almond paste into 16 pieces and pat each piece into a round disk about 1½ inches across.

In a large bowl, beat butter until creamy. Beat in sugar until pale and fluffy. Beat in eggs, one at a time, then mix in baking powder, baking soda, and almond extract.

With a rubber spatula fold in 1 cup of the flour, then the yogurt, and lastly the remaining flour until well blended.

Spoon about 2 tablespoons of batter into each cup and smooth surface with your fingers. Top with a level teaspoon of raspberry preserves, then with a piece of almond paste. Top each muffin with another 2 tablespoons of batter.

Bake 25 to 30 minutes, or until lightly browned. Turn out onto a rack and let stand at least 10 minutes.

RHUBARB MUFFINS

This is an unusual and delicious way to use fresh rhubarb, which is so plentiful in markets in the early spring. Works fine with frozen rhubarb too. Good with a dab of yogurt or sour cream. Or try them topped with Very Strawberry Butter (page 85). *Serve warm.*

1½ cups diced fresh rhubarb (discard leaves) or 2 cups frozen sliced rhubarb

2 cups all-purpose flour

1 tablespoon baking powder

¼ teaspoon salt

¼ teaspoon ground cinnamon

1 large egg

½ cup packed light brown sugar

3 tablespoons red currant jelly

1 cup milk

4 tablespoons (½ stick) butter, melted

1 teaspoon vanilla extract

If you are using frozen rhubarb, spread it on the counter for about 5 minutes until it is thawed enough to finely dice.

While rhubarb thaws, heat oven to 375° F. Grease muffin cups, or use paper or foil baking cups.

Thoroughly mix flour, baking powder, salt, and cinnamon in a large bowl.

In a medium-size bowl, whisk egg, brown sugar, and currant jelly until smooth (jelly will not completely dissolve). Whisk in milk, butter, and vanilla. Stir in finely diced rhubarb. Pour over dry ingredients and fold in with a rubber spatula just until dry ingredients are moistened.

Scoop batter into muffin cups. Bake 20 to 30 minutes, or until light brown and springy to the touch in the center. Turn out onto a rack and cool at least 15 minutes before serving.

SAVORY MUFFINS

MUFFINS BOURSIN

12 REGULAR OR 36 MINIATURE MUFFINS

Simply savory and redolent with garlic, these muffins are equally delicious with fish or chicken. They are also perfect for brunch, served with a puffy vegetable omelet. *Serve warm.*

1½ cups all-purpose flour
 ½ cup oat bran (see note, page 13)
 1 tablespoon baking powder
 ¾ teaspoon salt
 ¼ teaspoon freshly ground black pepper
 1 large egg
 1 5-ounce package Boursin cheese
 ¾ cup milk
 2 teaspoons snipped fresh chives or
    1 teaspoon freeze-dried chives

Heat oven to 350° F. Grease muffin cups, or use foil or paper baking cups.

Thoroughly mix flour, oat bran, baking powder, salt, and pepper in a large bowl.

Beat egg with a whisk or fork in a small bowl. Whisk in cheese until well broken up. Whisk in milk and chives. Pour over dry ingredients. Fold in with a rubber spatula until dry ingredients are moistened; batter will bubble and thicken.

Scoop batter into muffin cups. Bake about 30 minutes, for regular muffins, 17 to 20 minutes for miniature muffins, until a toothpick inserted in the center comes out clean. Turn out onto a rack to cool.

SOUR CREAM JALAPEÑO CORN MUFFINS

Wonderful with ribs or other barbecued meat. The larger amount of jalapeño makes a very peppery muffin. *Serve at any temperature.*

$1\frac{1}{2}$ cups yellow corn meal
 ½ cup all-purpose flour
 1 tablespoon granulated sugar
 1 tablespoon baking powder
 1 teaspoon salt
 2 large eggs
 1 cup sour cream
 *1 to $1\frac{1}{2}$ teaspoons minced, seeded,
    fresh or canned jalapeño pepper*

Heat oven to 350° F. Grease muffin cups, or use paper or foil baking cups.

Thoroughly mix corn meal, flour, sugar, baking powder, and salt in a large bowl.

Beat eggs and sour cream with a whisk or fork in a small bowl. When smooth, stir in jalapeño. Pour over flour mixture. Fold in with a rubber spatula until well mixed; batter will be very stiff.

Scoop batter into muffin cups. Bake 20 to 25 minutes, or until firm to the touch in the center. Let cool 5 minutes in pan before turning out onto a rack to cool.

VARIATION: For plain corn muffins, omit the jalapeño!

CRANBERRY APPLE MUFFINS

12 REGULAR MUFFINS

Turn your ordinary roast chicken or turkey dinner into a festive occasion. Instead of biscuits, heap these not too sweet muffins in a basket. *Make a day ahead for best flavor; serve warm.*

1 cup all-purpose flour
½ cup whole-wheat flour, oat bran, or
    all-purpose flour
1 teaspoon baking soda
1 teaspoon ground cinnamon
¼ teaspoon salt
2 large eggs
¾ cup packed dark brown sugar
¼ cup vegetable oil
1 teaspoon vanilla extract
¾ cup diced unpeeled tart apple
¾ cup fresh or frozen cranberries
½ cup chopped walnuts

Heat oven to 350° F. Grease muffin cups, or use foil cups.
Mix flours, baking soda, cinnamon, and salt in a large bowl.
Break eggs into another bowl. Add sugar and whisk until smooth. Whisk in oil and vanilla. Stir in apple, cranberries, and walnuts. Pour over dry ingredients. Fold in just until dry ingredients are moistened.

Scoop batter into muffin cups. Bake 20 to 25 minutes, or until browned and firm to the touch. Turn out onto a rack. Let cool. Store 1 to 2 days in a plastic bag or airtight container before reheating and serving. Do not freeze.

SMOKED-CHEESE AND
SCALLION MUFFINS

12 TO 14 REGULAR MUFFINS

When warm, the cheese in these muffins is stringy and fun to eat, but the flavor is more intense when the muffins have cooled completely. Great with soups. *Serve warm or at room temperature.*

 2 cups all-purpose flour
 1 tablespoon baking powder
 ¾ teaspoon salt
 ¼ to ½ teaspoon freshly ground black pepper
 ¼ teaspoon dried thyme leaves, crumbled
 1 large egg
 1 cup milk
 ½ cup chopped fresh tomato
 ¼ cup thinly sliced scallions
 4 ounces smoked Gouda, provolone, or
    mozzarella cheese, cut into ¼-inch dice
 4 tablespoons (½ stick) butter, melted

Heat oven to 375° F. Grease muffin cups; do not use paper or foil baking cups.

Thoroughly mix flour, baking powder, salt, pepper, and thyme in a large bowl.

Whisk egg and milk in a medium-size bowl. When egg is well broken up, stir in tomato, scallions, cheese, and butter.

Pour over dry ingredients and fold in with a rubber spatula just until dry ingredients are moistened.

Scoop batter into muffin cups. Bake 25 to 30 minutes, or until browned. Turn out onto a rack to cool.

CHEDDAR CHEESE AND MUSTARD MUFFINS

12 REGULAR OR 36 MINIATURE MUFFINS

Try these with sausages for a hearty supper, or with lentil or minestrone soup and a green salad. *Serve warm.*

2 cups all-purpose flour
1 tablespoon baking powder
½ teaspoon salt
⅛ teaspoon freshly ground black pepper
1 cup (4 ounces) coarsely grated
  extra-sharp Cheddar cheese
1 large egg
3 to 4 tablespoons spicy-hot prepared mustard
1 cup milk
¼ cup (½ stick) butter, melted

Heat oven to 350° F. Grease muffin cups, or use foil or paper baking cups.

Thoroughly mix flour, baking powder, salt, and pepper in a large bowl. Add cheese. Toss flour and cheese with fingers to distribute cheese evenly.

Whisk egg and mustard in a small bowl. When well mixed, whisk in milk and butter. Pour over flour mixture. Fold in gently with a rubber spatula, just until dry ingredients are moistened.

Scoop batter into muffin cups. Bake 20 to 25 minutes, or until springy to the touch in the center. Turn out onto rack to cool.

DOUBLE CORN AND
GREEN CHILE MUFFINS

Corn kernels as well as corn meal make these muffins especially moist. They are delicious as a snack with beer, or with a salad. *Serve hot or warm.*

1½ cups yellow corn meal
½ cup all-purpose flour
1 tablespoon baking powder
1 teaspoon salt
¼ teaspoon black pepper
2 large eggs
1 cup sour cream
¼ cup (½ stick) butter, melted
1 12-ounce can corn kernels, drained;
   or 3 cups frozen corn kernels, thawed
1 cup (4 ounces) coarsely grated sharp Cheddar cheese
¼ cup chopped canned green chilies

Heat oven to 350° F. Line regular muffin cups with foil baking cups, or put baking cups directly on a baking sheet.

Thoroughly mix corn meal, flour, baking powder, salt, and pepper in a large bowl.

Whisk eggs and sour cream in a medium-size bowl until smooth. Whisk in butter. Stir in corn, cheese, and chilies. Pour over dry ingredients and fold in with a rubber spatula until dry ingredients are moistened.

Scoop batter into muffin cups. Bake 25 to 30 minutes, or until no longer moist in the center. Let cool a few minutes before serving.

THYME AND ONION MUFFINS

12 REGULAR OR 36 MINIATURE MUFFINS

These taste like a wonderful herb stuffing, but they are quicker and easier to make. Serve with a juicy chicken, a casserole, or roast pork. *Serve warm.*

  4 *tablespoons (½ stick) butter*
 ½ *cup finely chopped onion*
 ¼ *teaspoon dried thyme or sage leaves*
1½ *cups all-purpose flour*
 ½ *cup oat bran (see note, page 13)*
  1 *tablespoon baking powder*
 ¾ *teaspoon salt*
 ⅛ *teaspoon pepper*
  1 *large egg*
  1 *cup milk*

Melt butter in a small saucepan over moderate heat. Add onion and cook 4 to 5 minutes, stirring several times until tender. Remove from heat. Crumble thyme leaves into the saucepan and stir into the butter.

Heat oven to 400° F. Grease muffin cups, or use foil or paper baking cups.

Thoroughly mix flour, oat bran, baking powder, salt, and pepper in a large bowl.

Beat egg in a small bowl; whisk in milk. Add onion and herb mixture. Pour over dry ingredients. Mix gently with a rubber spatula, just until dry ingredients are moistened.

Scoop batter into muffin cups. Bake 20 to 25 minutes, until tinged with brown and no longer damp in the center. Cool in pans 10 minutes before turning out onto a rack.

COTTAGE CHEESE AND DILL MUFFINS

S oft and moist, these muffins are superb for brunch or supper along with scrambled eggs or an omelet and a crisp, green salad. The larger amount of pepper makes a muffin that's, well, *peppery*. It's especially good with a salsa omelet. *Cool completely before serving.*

     2 cups all-purpose flour
     1 tablespoon granulated sugar
    2½ teaspoons baking powder
    1½ teaspoons dried dillweed
     ½ teaspoon salt
     ¼ to ½ teaspoon freshly ground
        black pepper
     1 large egg
     1 cup (8-ounce container) creamed
        small-curd cottage cheese
     ½ cup milk
     4 tablespoons (½ stick) butter,
        melted
    1½ tablespoons coarsely grated onion

Heat oven to 400° F. Line muffin cups with foil baking cups, or put foil baking cups directly onto a baking sheet. (Baking cups are essential for these muffins, since they tend to stick to pans of any kind.)

Thoroughly mix flour, sugar, baking powder, dillweed, salt, and pepper in a large bowl.

Beat egg in a medium-size bowl; whisk in cottage cheese, milk, melted butter, and onion. Pour over dry ingredients and fold in with a rubber spatula, just until dry ingredients are moistened.

Scoop batter into baking cups. Bake 15 to 20 minutes, or until springy to the touch in the center. Cool muffins completely on a rack before eating.

SMOKED TURKEY, WILD RICE, AND MUSHROOM MUFFINS

16 REGULAR OR 36 MINIATURE MUFFINS

What began for me as a refrigerator encounter with some cooked wild rice eventually grew into an intriguing and elegant muffin. It is superb with a Caesar salad and a wedge of Brie, or Muenster cheese. Top these muffins with Herb Butter (page 84). *Serve warm.*

  4 *tablespoons (½ stick) butter*
 ½ *cup finely chopped onion*
 ½ *teaspoon minced fresh garlic*
  1 *cup chopped mushrooms (3 or 4 medium-size)*
  2 *cups all-purpose flour*
  1 *tablespoon baking powder*
  1 *teaspoon salt*
 ½ *teaspoon freshly ground black pepper*
  1 *cup milk*
  2 *large eggs*
  1 *cup cooked wild rice (see note)*
  4 *ounces smoked turkey, chopped (¾ cup)*

In a medium-size heavy saucepan, melt butter over moderate heat. Add onion and garlic and cook 5 to 7 minutes, stirring occasionally until soft. Add mushrooms and cook 2 to 3 minutes longer. Remove from heat.

Heat oven to 350° F. Grease muffin cups, or use foil baking cups.

Thoroughly mix flour, baking powder, salt, and pepper in a large bowl.

Whisk milk and eggs in a medium-size bowl. Stir in wild rice, turkey, and mushroom mixture. Pour over dry ingredients. Fold in with a rubber spatula until dry ingredients are moistened; batter will be stiff.

Scoop batter into muffin cups. Bake 25 to 30 minutes, or until muffins are no longer moist in the center. Let cool in pans about 5 minutes before turning out onto a rack.

NOTE: To make 1 cup cooked wild rice, simmer ¼ cup wild rice in 1 cup water in a small, heavy covered saucepan for about 40 minutes, or until grains have burst open and are tender. Cool before using.

VARIATION: Use 4 ounces of smoked ham instead of turkey.

SPICY ITALIAN SAUSAGE MUFFINS

16 REGULAR OR 48 MINIATURE MUFFINS

Intensely flavorful and satisfying, these muffins go nicely with a crunchy salad. The miniature size makes a delicious appetizer that's incredibly easy to prepare. *Serve warm.*

2 sweet Italian sausages (7 to 8 ounces total)
2 cups all-purpose flour
⅓ cup grated Parmesan cheese
1 tablespoon baking powder
½ teaspoon salt
⅛ teaspoon freshly ground black pepper
½ teaspoon dried oregano leaves
1 large egg
1 14-ounce jar pizza sauce
About 2 tablespoons olive or vegetable oil

Remove sausages from casing, break them into pieces, and place in a skillet. Fry over moderate heat, stirring and breaking up sausage with a spoon until cooked and browned. While sausage cooks, heat oven to 400° F. Grease muffin cups, or use foil or paper baking cups. Drain sausage on a paper towel —save fat in skillet.

Thoroughly mix flour, Parmesan, baking powder, salt, and pepper in a large bowl. Crumble the oregano in your fingers to release the flavor and stir into flour mixture.

Break egg into a medium-size bowl. Lightly beat with a fork

or whisk; blend in pizza sauce. Add 3 tablespoons fat or oil to sauce mixture—start with fat from skillet and make up difference with olive or vegetable oil. Add sausage and mix well.

Pour sauce mixture over dry ingredients and mix gently with a rubber spatula until dry ingredients are moistened. Scoop the very thick batter into muffin cups. Bake 20 to 25 minutes, or until firm on top. Turn out onto a rack and cool at least 30 minutes before serving.

BACON MUFFINS

These muffins are delicious with a spinach salad, for lunch or brunch, or of course alongside eggs for breakfast. Good with Herb Butter (page 84). *Serve warm.*

- 4 *thick strips (5 ounces) bacon*
  Vegetable oil as needed
- 2 *cups all-purpose flour*
- 1 *tablespoon granulated sugar*
- 1 *tablespoon baking powder*
- 1 *teaspoon salt*
- ⅛ *teaspoon pepper (or more to taste)*
- 1 *large egg*
- 1 *cup milk*

While bacon is still very cold, stack the strips, cut them in 4 lengthwise and then cut them across in ½-inch pieces. Cook bacon in a small, heavy saucepan (about 6 inches in diameter) until light golden brown, but not crisp. Pour fat through a strainer set over a measuring cup; add vegetable oil if needed to bring fat up to the ¼-cup level. Drain bacon on paper towels.

While bacon cooks, heat oven to 400° F. Grease muffin cups, or use foil or paper baking cups.

Mix flour, sugar, baking powder, salt, and pepper in a large bowl.

Whisk egg, milk, and bacon fat in a small bowl until egg is well broken up. Add bacon and pour over dry ingredients. Fold in with a rubber spatula, just until dry ingredients are moistened.

Scoop batter into muffin cups. Bake 15 to 20 minutes, or until golden brown and springy to the touch in the center. Let cool in pans 5 minutes, then turn out onto a rack.

VARIATION:

BACON ONION MUFFINS. When bacon is almost done, add ½ cup finely chopped onion. Fry 4 to 5 minutes, stirring occasionally, until onion is translucent. Proceed as above except: Omit sugar; reduce salt to ¾ teaspoon. Add ½ teaspoon dry mustard and a pinch each thyme and ground red pepper (cayenne) to flour. Use plain yogurt or buttermilk instead of regular milk.

ENGLISH MUFFINS

ENGLISH MUFFINS

Although yeast, not baking powder, makes these rangetop muffins rise, you'll find they're well worth the wait. Serve with plain or Honey Butter (page 84), Quick Apricot Preserves (page 88), or Quick Rhubarb Strawberry Preserves (page 87).

1 teaspoon granulated sugar
1 cup warm water (105° to 115° F.)
1 envelope (1 tablespoon) active dried yeast
2 cups buttermilk
4 cups all-purpose flour
1 teaspoon salt
1 teaspoon baking soda
   Vegetable oil, for griddle
   Melted unsalted butter, for muffin rings

Fit electric mixer with dough hook or paddle. Put sugar and ¼ cup of the water in mixer bowl; sprinkle with yeast. Mix for a few seconds. Let stand a few minutes until yeast is foamy.

Heat buttermilk until it is barely warm to the touch; it will probably curdle but do not worry. When warm, remove from heat.

Measure flour; sprinkle over yeast. Add salt. Pour buttermilk over flour. Mix on low speed just to combine. Then beat 3 minutes on medium speed. Batter will be sticky and elastic.

Remove bowl from machine; cover with plastic wrap and let rise 1 hour in a warm place (70° to 80° F.), until bubbly and doubled in volume.

Dissolve baking soda in remaining ¾ cup warm water. Add to batter. Mix, then beat 1 minute. Cover bowl and let rise 30 minutes longer.

Heat electric skillet (for best results) to about 260° F.; or heat one or more iron skillets or griddles over moderately low heat. Brush heated skillet or griddle lightly with oil and place buttered 3-inch muffin rings (or clean tuna cans, open at both ends) on it. Using a buttered ¼-cup measure, scoop ¼ cup of the batter into each muffin ring, spreading with fingers until it touches sides of rings.

Cook muffins 7 to 10 minutes—they will rise to about ¾ inch, and bubbles will appear on the surface and break; raise or lower heat as necessary so muffins cook slowly and evenly and do not get too dark on the bottom. When muffins are golden brown on the bottom and almost dry on the top, remove the rings with tongs and turn the muffins over. Cook 7 to 10 minutes longer until the second side is browned.

Cool muffins at least 15 minutes on a wire rack. Split open with a fork and toast cut sides under a broiler.

NOTE: If you do not have a mixer with a paddle or dough hook, after stirring in the flour, beat mixture with a wooden spoon for about 3 minutes. After dough has risen, beat about 1 minute more.

WHOLE-WHEAT BRAN
ENGLISH MUFFINS

1 *tablespoon honey*
1 *cup warm water (105° to 115° F.)*
1 *envelope (1 tablespoon) active dried yeast*
2 *cups buttermilk*
2 *cups all-purpose flour*
2 *cups whole-wheat flour*
½ *cup unprocessed wheat bran (miller's bran)*
1 *teaspoon salt*
1 *teaspoon baking soda*

Follow the English Muffin recipe (page 67), using honey instead of sugar and adding the whole-wheat flour and bran along with the all-purpose flour.

VARIATIONS:

CINNAMON RAISIN MUFFINS. Follow the recipe for Whole-Wheat Bran English Muffins, adding 1 cup dark raisins and 1½ teaspoons ground cinnamon to the flour.

CORN-RYE ENGLISH MUFFINS. Follow the recipe for Whole-Wheat Bran English Muffins, using 3 cups all-purpose flour, 1 cup rye flour, and ¼ cup yellow corn meal (omit bran).

RAISIN-RYE ENGLISH MUFFINS. Follow the Corn-Rye English Muffin recipe above and add 1 cup golden raisins with the flour.

SPECIAL-DIET MUFFINS

LOW-CALORIE BLUEBERRY MUFFINS

12 REGULAR MUFFINS

Small blueberries work best. Try making these muffins with finely chopped peaches, plums, or raspberries. Only 107 calories in each blueberry muffin. *Serve hot or warm.*

¾ cup all-purpose flour
¾ cup whole-wheat flour
¼ cup granulated sugar
2 teaspoons baking powder
¼ teaspoon salt
1 large egg
½ cup skim milk
2 tablespoons unsalted butter or
   margarine, melted
1 cup blueberries
¼ teaspoon freshly grated lemon peel

Heat oven to 375° F. Grease muffin cups—or, to eliminate even the few calories from greasing, use foil or paper baking cups.

Thoroughly mix flours, sugar, baking powder, and salt in a large bowl.

Beat egg with a fork or whisk in a small bowl. Whisk in milk and butter. Pour over dry ingredients. Add berries and lemon peel. Fold in with a rubber spatula just until dry ingredients are moistened.

Scoop batter into muffin cups. Bake 15 to 20 minutes, or until lightly browned. Cool 5 minutes before removing from pans.

CALORIE-CONSCIOUS OAT MUFFINS

12 REGULAR OR 36 MINIATURE MUFFINS

These delicious muffins, in regular size, are only 115 calories each. *Let cool at least 2 hours after baking for the flavor to develop.*

¾ cup all-purpose flour
½ cup whole-wheat flour
¾ cup quick-cooking oats (not instant)
1 tablespoon baking powder
½ teaspoon ground cinnamon
¼ teaspoon ground ginger
¼ teaspoon salt
1 large egg
1 cup skim milk
2 tablespoons margarine or butter, melted
1 tablespoon honey
1 teaspoon vanilla extract
¾ cup finely chopped unpeeled sweet apple, such as golden Delicious
3 tablespoons raisins

Heat oven to 400° F. Grease muffin cups, or use paper baking cups.

Thoroughly mix flours, oats, baking powder, cinnamon, ginger, and salt in a large bowl.

Beat egg with a fork or whisk in a medium-size bowl. Whisk in milk, margarine, honey, and vanilla. Stir in apple and raisins. Pour over dry ingredients and fold in with a rubber spatula just until dry ingredients are moistened.

Scoop batter into cups. Bake 20 minutes, or until lightly browned.

WHEAT-FREE BANANA MUFFINS

Use very ripe bananas, those with lots of brown flecks in the skin. Rice flour can be found in health food stores or in stores carrying Spanish groceries. *Serve warm, but make a day ahead for best flavor.*

1½ cups rice flour
 ½ cup quick-cooking oats (not instant)
2½ teaspoons baking powder
 ½ teaspoon baking soda
 ½ teaspoon ground nutmeg
 ¼ teaspoon salt
 2 large ripe bananas, mashed (1 cup)
 ¼ cup vegetable oil
 ¼ cup honey
 ¼ cup warm water
 1 large egg
 1 teaspoon vanilla extract

Heat oven to 400° F. Grease muffin cups, or use foil or paper baking cups.

Thoroughly mix rice flour, oats, baking powder, baking soda, nutmeg, and salt in a large bowl.

Put remaining ingredients in a medium-size bowl. Beat with a fork or whisk until well blended. Pour over dry ingredients and fold in with a rubber spatula just until dry ingredients are moistened.

Scoop batter into muffin cups. Bake 20 minutes, or until golden. Place pan on a wire rack to cool 5 to 10 minutes before turning muffins out.

WHEAT-FREE GINGERBREAD MUFFINS

12 REGULAR MUFFINS

Although these do not taste very good hot, you'll be amazed at how wonderful the flavor is after an hour or so. These are also low-sodium. *Cool at least 1 hour before serving.*

¾ cup brown rice flour or potato starch
½ teaspoon ground cinnamon
½ teaspoon ground ginger
⅛ teaspoon ground cloves
   Yolks of 2 large eggs
2 tablespoons light molasses (see note)
½ teaspoon freshly grated orange peel
2 tablespoons freshly squeezed orange juice
   Whites of 4 large eggs
2 tablespoons granulated sugar
¼ cup freshly squeezed lemon juice
   mixed with 2 tablespoons granulated sugar (optional)

Heat oven to 400° F. Grease muffin cups, or use foil baking cups. Mix rice flour and spices in a large bowl.

Put egg yolks, molasses, orange peel, and orange juice in a small bowl; whisk with a fork to mix. Add to dry ingredients and stir gently until well blended; batter will be stiff and difficult to mix.

In a deep, medium-size bowl, beat egg whites with a rotary beater or electric mixer until soft peaks form when beater is lifted. Beat in sugar 1 tablespoon at a time, until whites are thick and glossy.

Stir about one fourth of the beaten whites into the rice flour batter to lighten it, then fold in the remainder. Scoop batter into muffin cups and bake 15 to 20 minutes, or until golden brown and springy to the touch. Turn out onto a rack and cool 10 minutes. Brush tops with, or dip them in, lemon juice mixture. Let cool at least 50 minutes longer.

NOTE: Do not use blackstrap molasses. It has a high sodium content and the flavor is too strong.

LOW-SODIUM MAPLE PECAN MUFFINS

16 REGULAR OR 48 MINIATURE MUFFINS

There's no baking powder or baking soda in these delicious maple muffins. Instead, when the air beaten into the egg whites expands in the heat of the oven, the muffins rise. In regular size, these muffins are approximately 111 calories with 18 milligrams of sodium in each. *Cool 10 minutes before serving.*

 1 cup all-purpose flour
 ½ cup whole-wheat flour
 ¼ cup chopped pecans
    Yolks of 2 large eggs
 ½ cup milk
 ¼ cup maple syrup
 2 tablespoons unsalted butter or
    margarine, melted
    Whites of 4 large eggs
 3 tablespoons granulated sugar

Heat oven to 400° F. Grease muffin cups, or use foil or paper baking cups.

Mix flours and pecans in a large bowl. Put egg yolks, milk, maple syrup, and melted butter into a medium-size bowl.

Put egg whites into another medium-size bowl. Beat with an electric mixer at high speed (or with a rotary beater) until soft peaks form when beater is lifted. Add sugar 1 tablespoon at a time, beating well after each addition. Whites should be glossy and very white and form stiff peaks.

Use the same beater (no need to wash) to beat milk mixture until well blended.

Pour milk mixture over dry ingredients. Fold in with a rubber spatula until dry ingredients are fairly well moistened. Scrape beaten egg whites over the top; fold in gently, just until blended.

Fill muffin cups almost to the top with the batter. Bake about 20 minutes or until lightly browned. Cool in pan on a wire rack for 10 minutes before turning muffins out.

LOW-CHOLESTEROL CARROT ORANGE MUFFINS

12 REGULAR OR 36 MINIATURE MUFFINS

These delicate, flavorful muffins use egg whites instead of whole eggs; vegetable oil replaces butter and skim milk replaces whole milk. Delicious for tea time, each regular muffin has less than 1 milligram of cholesterol. *Serve hot.*

1 *cup unbleached all-purpose flour*
1 *cup whole-wheat flour*
2 *teaspoons baking powder*
1 *teaspoon ground cinnamon*
¼ *teaspoon salt*
1 *teaspoon freshly grated orange peel*
½ *cup plus 2 tablespoons orange juice,*
    preferably freshly squeezed
½ *cup skim milk*
¼ *cup vegetable oil*
2 *tablespoons honey*
    Whites of 2 large eggs
1 *cup coarsely grated carrot*

Heat oven to 400° F. Grease muffin cups, or use foil or paper baking cups.

Thoroughly mix flours, baking powder, cinnamon, and salt in a large bowl.

Put orange peel, orange juice, milk, oil, honey, and egg whites in a medium-size bowl. Beat with a fork or whisk until egg whites are well broken up (the mixture will have a curdled look). Stir in the carrot. Pour over dry ingredients and fold in with a rubber spatula just until dry ingredients are moistened.

Scoop batter into muffin cups. Bake 20 to 25 minutes, or until lightly browned. Place pan on a wire rack to cool for a few minutes before removing muffins.

VARIATION: For low-cholesterol zucchini orange muffins, use 1 cup coarsely grated zucchini instead of the carrot.

ORANGE CURRANT OAT MUFFINS

12 REGULAR MUFFINS

These wheat-free, milk-free, and cholesterol-free, high-fiber muffins are good for corn-free diets too if corn-free baking powder and oil are used. The combination of orange juice, orange zest, and currants makes these muffins particularly delicious. *Serve warm.*

2¼ cups oat bran (see note, page 13)
 ½ cup *Zante currants*
 1 tablespoon baking powder
 1 teaspoon freshly grated orange peel
 ⅓ cup granulated sugar
 ½ cup freshly squeezed orange juice
 ¼ cup vegetable oil
   Whites of 3 large eggs

Heat oven to 375° F. Grease muffin cups, or use foil baking cups.

Thoroughly mix oat bran, currants, baking powder, orange peel, and about ¼ cup of the sugar in a large bowl. Add orange juice and oil and stir until well blended.

In a small, deep bowl, beat egg whites with a rotary beater or electric mixer until soft peaks form when beater is lifted. Add remaining sugar and beat until whites are thick and glossy.

Stir about one fourth of the whites into the oat mixture to lighten it. Fold in remainder.

Scoop batter into muffin cups. Bake about 20 minutes, or until golden brown. Turn out onto a rack to cool.

SIDNEY BURSTEIN'S PASSOVER MATZO MEAL MUFFINS

12 REGULAR OR 36 MINIATURE MUFFINS

Soft and moist, a cross between muffins and popovers, these delicate puffs fill the need for an unleavened bread for Passover. Delicious served warm with Honey Butter (page 84) or Smoked Fish Spread (below). *Serve warm or at room temperature.*

- 1 *cup water*
- ½ *cup butter or margarine*
- ½ *teaspoon salt*
- 1 *cup unsalted matzo meal*
- 5 *large eggs*

Bring water, butter, and salt to a boil in a heavy, 2-quart saucepan, stirring to melt butter.

Remove from heat; immediately pour in all the matzo meal and stir with a wooden spoon to make a smooth paste. Add eggs, one at a time, beating briefly after each addition.

Heat oven to 400° F. Grease muffin cups (do not use paper baking cups). Fill miniature pans with about 1 tablespoon batter, regular muffin cups with about ¼ cup batter. Bake about 15 or 35 minutes, or until browned and puffed. Turn muffins out onto a rack. These muffins freeze and reheat well.

SMOKED FISH SPREAD

Place carefully boned fish from an 8-ounce smoked whiting (or other smoked fish) with ¼ cup (½ stick) unsalted margarine or butter, at room temperature, in a food processor. Process a few seconds to make a smooth paste. Add pepper if desired. Serve right away, or refrigerate up to 3 days.

SPREADS & PRESERVES

QUICK HOT PEPPER JELLY

ABOUT ½ CUP

$\mathbb{T}$his jelly is good with plain and savory muffins such as corn muffins. Southerners like a dab of it on cream cheese spread on crackers. *Keeps several weeks in the refrigerator.*

1 *small green pepper, cored, seeded, and quartered*
½ *to 1 small whole fresh or pickled jalapeño pepper, halved and seeded*
2 *tablespoons apple cider vinegar*
5 *ounces apple jelly (½ a 10-ounce jar)*

Put peppers and vinegar in a blender or a food processor. Purée as smooth as possible.

Put apple jelly in a 3- to 4-quart heavy pot (with a nonstick or stainless finish). Melt jelly over moderate heat. Add pepper purée. Stir until boiling. Reduce heat to moderately low and simmer about 7 minutes, stirring frequently, until thick, syrupy, and jellylike. During this time, taste the jelly (caution: it is very hot). Add 1 more teaspoon cider vinegar if you wish. Pour into a jar or serving bowl. Cover and refrigerate.

HONEY BUTTER

ABOUT ⅓ CUP

H oney butter is delicious on just about any bread from toast to pancakes; it's especially flavorful on Bran Muffins (page 14), Banana and The Best Blueberry Muffins (page 11). Try different honeys too! *Keeps indefinitely in the refrigerator.*

4 tablespoons unsalted butter, at
   room temperature
1 tablespoon honey

Beat butter and honey in a small bowl until fluffy and well mixed. Store tightly covered.

HERB BUTTER

ABOUT ½ CUP

T his spread is best made with fresh herbs, even if you have only parsley and chives. With dried herbs, use fresh parsley as a base and about ½ teaspoon of dried thyme, dill, or marjoram. Crumble the dried herbs between your fingers as you add them to release the flavor. *Keeps at least two weeks in the refrigerator.*

½ cup butter, at room temperature
 2 to 4 tablespoons chopped fresh parsley

*1 to 2 tablespoons chopped mixed
fresh chives, dill, savory, thyme, or
oregano—whatever you have
Salt and pepper to taste*

Beat the butter in a small bowl with a wooden spoon until creamy. Beat in 2 tablespoons of the parsley and about 2 teaspoons of the other herbs. Taste the butter—add more parsley and herbs, plus salt and pepper, to taste.

VERY STRAWBERRY BUTTER

ABOUT ½ CUP

Serve with bran or mixed-grain muffins. Store this, and all flavored butters, tightly covered, in the refrigerator. *Keeps at least one month.*

*4 tablespoons (½ stick) unsalted
butter, at room temperature
2 to 2½ tablespoons strawberry preserves, or
3 tablespoons low-sugar strawberry spread*

Beat butter with a wooden spoon in a small bowl; butter must be very soft and creamy, almost as soft as sour cream.

Beat in preserves 1 tablespoon at a time. By the third tablespoon the butter will acquire a curdled look; not to worry.

Put strawberry butter into a serving bowl and refrigerate. Let it soften at room temperature, without stirring, before serving.

NOTE: The calorie count is slightly lower when the low-sugar preserves are used and the flavor is more intense.

LEMON SPREAD

Τhis traditional English spread is wonderful with Nutmeg Muffins (page 40) or any bran muffin. It's also excellent as a cake filling. *Keeps at least two months in the refrigerator.*

  4 *large eggs*
 ¾ *cup granulated sugar*
1½ *tablespoons freshly grated lemon peel*
 ½ *cup freshly squeezed lemon juice*
  6 *tablespoons unsalted butter, cut
      into 12 pieces*

Beat eggs with a stainless steel whisk in the top of a double boiler or in a medium-size stainless steel bowl. Whisk in sugar, lemon peel, and juice. Place over simmering water. Check to make sure the water isn't touching the bottom of the double-boiler insert or bowl; otherwise, mixture may get too hot and curdle. Stir mixture constantly with a wooden spoon, until it is hot to the touch.

Add butter one piece at a time, stirring until each piece is melted—this should take 8 to 12 minutes.

When mixture is glossy, translucent, and creamy, remove from heat (see note). Pour into a serving dish, or into two clean, dry, hot, ½-pint jars. Let cool about 1 hour. Cover tightly and store in refrigerator.

NOTE: If you have a candy thermometer, use it. The mixture is ready when the thermometer reads 145° F.

QUICK RHUBARB STRAWBERRY PRESERVES

T*art and delicious, these preserves are particularly good with English Muffins (page 67). Keeps several weeks in the refrigerator.*

1 *pound rhubarb (discard leaves), cut
   into 1-inch slices; or 1 1-pound
   package frozen sliced rhubarb*
1 *10-ounce jar red currant jelly*
1 *pint small strawberries, washed,
   hulled, and sliced*

Put rhubarb and jelly in a large, heavy, 3- to 4-quart pot with a nonstick or stainless steel finish. Bring to a boil over high heat, stirring frequently. Reduce heat to moderately low, cover, and simmer 8 to 10 minutes, stirring occasionally until rhubarb is tender.

Remove from heat. Mash rhubarb with a slotted spoon or potato masher. Add strawberries. Bring to a full, rolling boil over high heat; boil 1 minute. Remove from heat. Pour into four, clean, dry, hot ½-pint jars. Cover and store in refrigerator.

QUICK APRICOT PRESERVES

ABOUT 2 CUPS

This spread is excellent with bran or banana nut muffins and with any relatively plain muffin, such as the Four-Grain Muffins (page 21). *Keeps several weeks in the refrigerator.*

-   1 8-ounce package (2 cups) dried
       apricot halves, cut in half
-   2 cups water
-   1 cup granulated sugar
-   2 tablespoons freshly squeezed lemon
       juice
-   ½ cup slivered blanched almonds,
       toasted if desired (optional)

Put apricots and water in a rather large, heavy saucepan, about 3- to 4-quart, that has a stainless or nonstick finish. Bring to a boil over high heat. Reduce heat to moderately high and boil 5 minutes. Remove from heat, cover, and let stand 30 minutes; most of the liquid will be absorbed.

Stir in sugar and lemon juice. Bring to a boil over moderate heat. Reduce heat to low and cook 10 to 15 minutes, mashing apricots occasionally with the back of a wooden spoon, until mixture is soft, syrupy, and thick—full of chunky pieces of apricot.

Remove from heat. Stir in almonds. Put preserves into a bowl, or two clean, dry, hot ½-pint jars. Cover and store in refrigerator.

INDEX